Illustrated
Stories *from the* Bible

Volume 5

AUTHORS
George and Marilyn Durrant
Former Professor of Ancient Scriptures

Educational Doctorate

ARTIST AND ART DIRECTOR
Vernon Murdock
Artist Illustrator

Bachelor of Fine Arts
Graduate Work, University of Madrid,
*   Spain*

CORRELATORS AND DIRECTORS
Steven R. Shallenberger, *President*
Community Press, Wisdom House, Eagle
*   Marketing Corporation*

Bachelor of Science; Accounting, Business.
SCMP, Graduate School of Business, Harvard
*   University.*

Paul R. Cheesman
Director of Scripture in Religious Study Center
Chaplain, U.S. Navy

Doctor of Religious Education

Lael J. Woodbury
Chairman, National Committee on Royalties,
*   American Theatre Association*

Doctorate of Theater, University of Illinois

ADVISORS
Dale T. Tingey
Director American Indian Services and
*   Research Center*

Doctor of Philosophy, Guidance and
*   Counseling; Washington State University*

Reverend Raymond E. Ansel
Ordained Minister

Southwestern Assemblies of God College, Texas
*   Berean Bible School, Missouri*

Millie Foster Cheesman
Writer, Poetess

M.J. Bardon
Missionary-Pastor, Grace Baptist Church

Th. M. Clarksville School of Theology
*   Clarksville, Tennessee*

Reverend William R. Schroeder
United Church of Christ

United Theological Seminary of the Twin Cities
*   New Brighton, Minnesota*

Copyright © 1980 by
EAGLE SYSTEMS INTERNATIONAL
Library of Congress Catalog Card No.: 80-80314
ISBN: 0-911712-65-8

FIRST EDITION VOLUME 5, 1981

Lithographed in U.S.A.
by
COMMUNITY PRESS, INC.
P.O. Box 1229
Antioch, California 94509

A Member of
The American Bookseller's Association
New York, New York

AND the LORD said unto Samuel . . . I will send thee to Jesse the Bethlehemite: for I have provided me a king among his sons . . . and thou shalt anoint unto me him whom I name unto thee.

And Samuel did that which the LORD spake, and came to Bethlehem. . . .

And it came to pass, when they were come, that he looked on Eliab, and said, Surely the LORD's anointed is before him.

But the LORD said unto Samuel, Look not on his countenance, or on the height of his stature; because I have refused him: for the LORD seeth not as man seeth; for man looketh on the outward appearance, but the LORD looketh on the heart. . . .

Again, Jesse made seven of his sons to pass before Samuel. And Samuel said unto Jesse, The LORD hath not chosen these. . . . And he [Jesse] said, There remaineth yet the youngest, and, behold, he keepeth the sheep. And Samuel said. . . . Send and fetch him. . . . And he sent, and brought him in. . . . And the LORD said, Arise, anoint him: for this is he.

. . . and the Spirit of the LORD came upon David from that day forward.

I Samuel 16:1-13

Dedicated to boys and girls throughout the world and to all who love the Bible.

A nondenominational work.

CONTENTS

Our story so far 7

True Friends *(David and Jonathan)* 8

Return Good for Evil *(Saul Dislikes David)* 15

Sickness of the Heart *(Saul's Last Days)* 18

The Promise Fulfilled *(David Becomes King)* 24

Temptation *(David and Bathsheba)* 30

A Troublesome Son *(Absalom)* 42

We Love Him *(David's Death)* 48

The Gift of Wisdom *(Solomon's Wisdom)* 52

A Wise Judge *(Solomon as a Judge)* 54

Fulfilling a Dream *(The Temple)* 60

Humility and Wisdom *(Solomon Begins to Lose)* 68

Pleasing People Rather Than the Lord *(Solomon's Wives)* 71

Love and Happiness to Misery *(Solomon's Reign Ends)* 74

Wanted: A Strong Leader *(The Birth of Elijah)* 76

The Mission Begins *(Elijah's Mission)* 78

Never-ending Food *(The Generous Widow)* 84

From Death to Life *(A Child Brought Back to Life)* 88

The Contest *(Elijah and the Priests of Baal)* 92

The Mission Ends *(Elisha)* 107

The Rich or the Poor *(Amos)* 123

Preview of Volume Six 135

Our story so far . . .

Thus far we have learned of the creation of this beautiful earth and of the first two people to live upon it—Adam and Eve. We thrilled at the courage of Noah and his mighty ark, and we traveled with Abraham to the Promised Land.

We read of Joseph and how he chose the right things. Later came the story of Moses, who led his people to the Promised Land. The walls of Jericho fell and Joshua and the Israelites began to conquer enemy armies.

Next we considered the rise and fall of Saul, and then we met David, the giant killer.

In this volume Saul becomes jealous of David and seeks to take his life. Saul's last days are unhappy ones. David becomes a mighty king of Israel and the people of God finally become a great people in their Promised Land.

Then David falls in love with Bathsheba and makes a terrible mistake. Because Bathsheba is married, David sends her husband to battle, knowing that this innocent man will be killed. He *is* killed and this great sin changes David's life from one of happiness to one of sorrow. He loses part of his kingdom and his own son tries to kill him. Then this son dies a horrible death and David's heart is broken.

Solomon, another of David's sons, becomes a wise king of Israel and people come from afar to see his beautiful kingdom. Solomon marries many women and becomes more interested in pleasing them than God. The Israelites divide into two kingdoms—the kingdom of Israel in the north and the kingdom of Judah in the south.

The mighty prophet Elijah then boldly enters the scene. He holds back the rain, is fed by birds, raises the dead, and defeats the priests of Baal in a contest of faith.

Elisha replaces Elijah and Israel returns to the worship of the true and living God.

The overall story of this volume will thrill us and build our faith in the power of the God of Israel—the only true and living God.

TRUE FRIENDS
I Samuel Chapters 18-20

At first Saul admired David because of his greatness. Then the old king became jealous because the people considered David such a hero. In one incident Saul lost his temper at David and angrily threw a

spear at him. Being very quick and athletic, David jumped to one side, and the sharp spear flew against a stone wall. As Saul frantically looked for another weapon, David escaped through an open door and ran into a nearby forest.

That night as David tried to sleep, his worried mind was filled with many thoughts and questions: "Why did the king do what he did? I have done nothing but love him and serve him. I am married to his daughter Michal. His son Jonathan and I are true friends. Why then does he hate me? Why does he want to kill me?"

Several days later David left his hiding place and secretly returned to a place near the home of Saul. There he met his friend Jonathan. As they talked, David was told that Saul was still angry. The two friends knew that David must go away and they should never see each other again. After they had embraced and wept, Jonathan said, "Go in peace. . . ." (I Samuel 20:42) They promised one another that their friendship would be forever. David then quickly turned and departed and Jonathan sadly returned to his father's house.

Even though he was King Saul's son, Jonathan did not wish to be king. He longed for the day when his friend David would be king. Yet when that day came, Jonathan would have already died at his father's side, having fought in a mighty battle against the Philistines. Although Jonathan's best friend was David, he also loved and remained loyal to his father, Saul.

Because he was good, unselfish, brave, and loyal, both to David and to his father, the name of Jonathan will forever signify a true and loyal friend. There could not have been a closer friendship than that which was shared by David and Jonathan.

THINK ABOUT IT

1. How did Jonathan teach us what a true friend is?
2. Which is better—to have a friend or to be a friend? Why?

RETURN GOOD FOR EVIL
I Samuel Chapter 24

David hid from Saul in the mountains. Others who had problems with the government of Saul joined David. In all there were several hundred people in David's camp. They had to be very careful because Saul spent much of his time trying to find and kill David.

Twice while Saul was in the mountains searching for David, David found Saul asleep and could have killed him. But he remembered the times when Saul had been good to him, so he did not harm Saul. Besides, he was married to Saul's daughter and David's children would be Saul's grandchildren. Also, Saul's son Jonathan was his best friend. David wished with all his heart that Saul would change back to how he had been when he was first chosen king.

One night while Saul and his soldiers slept in a cave, David quietly came into their camp. He came near to the sleeping king and cut off part of his royal robe. Saul did not awaken. The next morning David stood on top of a nearby hill and shouted, awakening Saul and his men. David explained what he had done and showed the cloth to prove his story.

Realizing that David could have killed him, Saul felt ashamed for his

hatred toward David. He spoke, "Thou *art* more righteous than I: for thou hast rewarded me good, whereas I have rewarded thee evil." Saul said other kind things and then added, "And now, behold, I know well that thou shalt surely be king. . . ." (I Samuel 24:17, 20)

This was a happy moment for David. Saul departed with his army and David began to prepare for what he believed would be a brighter future.

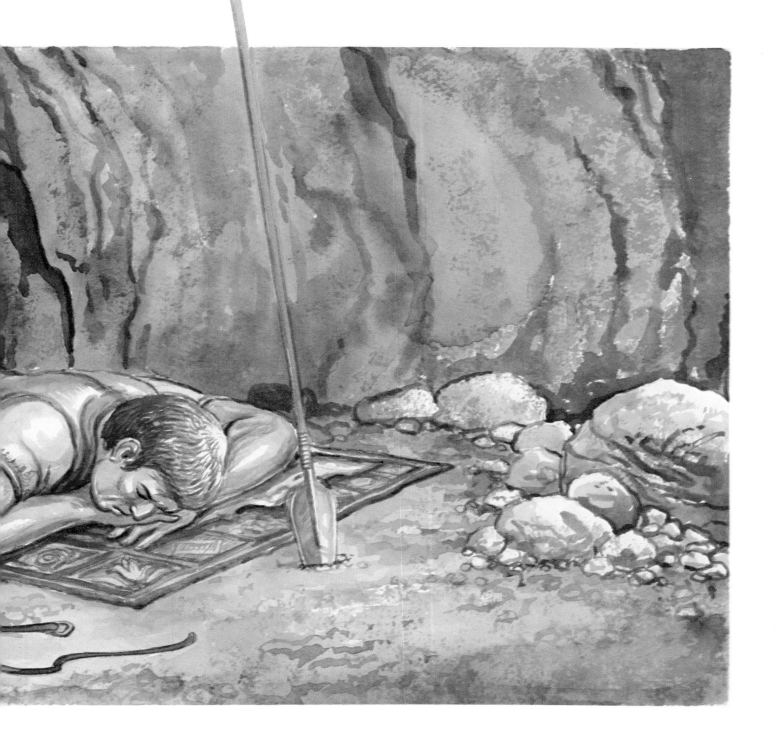

SICKNESS OF THE HEART
I Samuel Chapters 28-31

As Saul was returning home, Satan once again tempted him by putting strange ideas into his mind. Perhaps one of his captains said, "I think you made a mistake. David is not worthy and should never be king. You are the king, not him. You should return and kill him." Soon Saul's feelings changed and once again he began to feel anger towards David.

Sometimes when we let our hearts become filled with jealousy and hate, Satan uses this as a chance to make us more unhappy. Saul had been a good man, but the bad feelings which he had allowed to grow in his heart turned him away from goodness. As time went by, he turned more and more from the teachings of the Lord until finally he had turned away completely.

19

By this time the old king, who had now reigned for forty years, was most unhappy and confused. As he thought about his plans for the future, he remembered how he had received good ideas from the prophet Samuel in the past. Saul needed such help now, but since he could not go to Samuel, he went to a witch (a person who talks to evil spirits). Saul felt no better after talking to this witch for, among other things, he learned he would soon be killed.

Not long afterward Saul and his son Jonathan were engaged in a mighty war with the Philistines. "And the battle went sore against Saul, and the archers hit him; and he was sore wounded of the archers." (I Samuel 31:3) The badly injured king begged his armor bearer to kill him, but the young man would not. Saul then took his sword and, pointing it into his body, fell upon the sharp blade and died. David's dear friend Jonathan was also killed in the same battle.

If only Saul had been more obedient and had listened to Samuel. If only he had not been jealous of David. If only he had really changed when he said he would. There are so many "ifs." We each face many crossroads at which God invites us to come one way and Satan the other. The way we choose to go makes all the difference. Saul chose the evil way and Satan rejoiced. We can well imagine that God, along with David, wept at the sad ending to the life of one who could have been a great man.

THINK ABOUT IT

1. Do you feel sorry for Saul?
2. Why do you think he became so bitter and unhappy?

THE PROMISE FULFILLED

Much had happened since Samuel told David he would someday become king. Many times David had come close to losing his life. He may have wondered if he ever really would become the king of Israel. Still, deep within he had Samuel's assurance, and he must have thought to himself, "I must live worthily, I must have faith and be ready when the time comes. God has told me that I will be king, and I know that what he has promised will be fulfilled."

With the death of Saul the time had now come. David had been faithful and God was ready to fulfill his promise. Thus, at age thirty David became king over Israel.

David wanted his kingdom to be great, and he wanted the capital city to be Jerusalem, which was the foremost city in all the Promised Land at that time. There was one major problem with this desire—Jerusalem was in the hands of an enemy nation, the Jebusites.

The Jebusites boasted that David and his armies could never capture Jerusalem, which sat on top of a mountain. But they didn't understand the powers of God. David's forces attacked and soon were triumphant. Thereafter the mighty city of Jerusalem became known as the city of David.

The former shepherd boy was now a fine king who loved God with all his heart. He knew that God was the one who made all good things possible. To honor God, David had the priests bring the ark of the covenant, which had been in Israel's possession since the days of Moses, from a nearby city to Jersusalem. With the arrival of this sacred treasure the city of David, or Jerusalem, became a holy city.

To hear the name "King David" brought joy into the hearts of all the people of Israel. He was kind and ruled with wisdom, justice, and love. The people returned his love. David was so good at this time that God called him "a man after his own heart."

TEMPTATION
II Samuel Chapters 11, 12

As was the custom in those days, David had several wives. Two of these were Michal, Saul's daughter, and Abigail, whom he had married while hiding in the mountains. Thus, David became the father of many children.

Satan was not pleased that things were going well for the people of Israel and for David. He sought a way to destroy the plans of God. The Bible tells what happened. "And it came to pass in an eveningtide, that David arose from off his bed, and walked upon the roof of the king's house: and from the roof he saw a woman washing herself; and the woman *was* very beautiful to look upon." (II Samuel 11:2)

Thus began David's temptation. David felt that he must have
this woman, Bathsheba, to be his
wife. The great problem was that
she was already married to a man
named Uriah.

Then an idea came into David's mind that was not pleasing to God. He sent Uriah to the battlefront where the war was still being fought against the Philistines. David wrote Uriah's captain a letter, which said, "Set ye Uriah in the forefront of the hottest battle, and retire ye [move away] from him, that he may be smitten, and die." (II Samuel 11:15) The captain did as he was commanded and Uriah was killed in battle.

David was then free to marry Bathsheba (the dead man's wife). Up until this time he had been a good man and had kept the commandments of God. But now he had done a most wicked thing and must have felt at least some shame and unhappiness from his deed.

34

He may have thought: "I know I have done wrong; but no one else knows, so perhaps I will feel better soon and things will be alright again."

David was mistaken, for someone else did know that he had done wrong. God knew, and someone else also knew. There was at that time a new prophet in Israel, a man named Nathan. God spoke to this holy man and told him what David had done.

Shortly thereafter the prophet visited David, who must have wondered with concern, "Does this prophet know?" Nathan then told David a story: "There were two men in one city; the one rich, and the other poor." (II Samuel 12:1) Continuing on, he said, "A traveler came and asked the rich man for food. Instead of killing one of his own many lambs, he took the poor man's only lamb, killed it, and gave it to the traveler."

David was angry with what he was hearing and spoke out, "As the LORD liveth, the man that hath done this *thing* shall surely die." (II Samuel 12:5) The prophet stood closer to David. With a most serious expression on his face, he pointed his finger at David and said in a firm voice, "Thou *art* the man. . . ." (II Samuel 12:7)

David realized then that the prophet knew of the wicked, terrible thing he had done. He, the great king who had wanted so much to always be a friend of God, knew that his life would never again be the same. He had once dreamed of building a temple to God, but now he knew that God would not allow him to do that. He was no longer worthy.

David cried bitter tears and begged God for forgiveness. His life, which had been so happy in the past, was now filled with sorrow and regret. As time passed, the pain in his soul continued.

A son of David, born to Bathsheba, became ill and died. David felt that his heart would surely break. He wondered, "Will there ever be hope for me again?" He wrote many songs, or psalms as they are called in the Bible, about his feelings.

The Lord knew that David had suffered terribly and was truly sorry for what he had done. Our Father in heaven is merciful and understanding. If those who have disobeyed him will come unto him with a broken heart, and if they will strive from that time on to love and serve him, he will make it possible for many of them to be forgiven.

He can do this because he has sent us a Savior, who has paid the price for our sins. This is the Savior that Adam and Eve longed for when they had to leave the Garden of Eden. Moses knew of this Savior when he placed the bronze serpent on a pole and told the Israelites to look at it and they would be healed.

We all make mistakes, although most of us commit far less serious sins than David. Yet anyone who has a broken heart and follows all the things the Savior teaches can be forgiven.

We love David not because of the mistakes he made,
but because of the life he led before he disobeyed God.

A TROUBLESOME SON
II Samuel Chapters 15-18

As the years passed, David's life was filled with problems. Finally Absalom, one of his own sons, led a rebellion against him. Many of David's people turned against him and followed Absalom, thus forcing the king to flee from Jerusalem.

Soon there was a great civil war, as the army of Absalom marched forth to fight against the army of David. There were many who were still loyal to David, and his army began to win. Sensing that his son's army was going to be defeated, David said to his captains, "*Deal* gently for my sake with the young man, *even* with Absalom." (II Samuel 18:5)

Seeing his army being crushed, Absalom jumped onto the back of a mule and fled for his life. But the animal darted into some trees with low-hanging branches. As Absalom's long hair caught on a limb, he was jerked from the mule, and there he hung helplessly by his hair.

David's forces disobeyed his command to deal gently with his son. When they saw Absalom dangling helplessly by his hair, they came forth and quickly killed him.

They threw him into a pit and covered him over with rocks. For many years thereafter those who passed this place threw more rocks upon the grave, showing their disapproval of children who disobey their parents.

David was once again heartbroken. He knew his son had led a rebellion against him and would have killed him if he could have; but he also remembered Absalom as a little boy and a young man, and he loved him dearly. He cried, saying, "O my son Absalom, my son, my son Absalom! would God I had died for thee, O Absalom, my son, my son!" (II Samuel 18:33)

THINK ABOUT IT

What does this story teach us about the love parents have for their children?

WE LOVE HIM
I Kings 1, 2; Psalm 23

It is no wonder that we love David, a man who would rather have died than to have seen his son die. We are inspired by his beautiful writings in the Book of Psalms, where he wrote:

THE LORD *is* my shepherd; I shall not want.

He maketh me to lie down in green pastures: he leadeth me beside the still waters.

He restoreth my soul: he leadeth me in the paths of righteousness for his name's sake.

Yea, though I walk through the valley of the shadow of death, I will fear no evil: for thou *art* with me; thy rod and thy staff they comfort me.

Thou preparest a table before me in the presence of mine enemies: thou anointest my head with oil; my cup runneth over.

Surely goodness and mercy shall follow me all the days of my life: and I will dwell in the house of the LORD for ever.

(Psalm 23)

As we think about the life of David, we are inspired by the courage he showed in facing and defeating a giant. We are reminded to think of others when we read of his unselfishness. We are grateful that through his family line the Savior was born. David was beloved of the Lord, and the Lord called him "a man after his own heart." (I Samuel 13:14; Acts 13:22)

After many years had passed and David had grown old, he promised Bathsheba that their son Solomon would be the new king. Finally ". . . David slept with his fathers, and was buried in the city of

David. And the days that David reigned over Israel *were* forty years. . . ."
(I Kings 2:10, 11)

David taught us a great deal, for which we should be grateful and cherish his memory.

THINK ABOUT IT

1. What is a great lesson that we can learn from David's life?
2. Does sorrow only come to those who sin?

THE GIFT OF WISDOM
I Kings Chapter 3

If you could make one wish and have it granted, what would you wish for? After David died, his son Solomon was invited by the Lord to make such a wish. At the time Solomon was only about twenty years old and had just become king over all Israel. One night after praying to the Lord about his desire to be a good leader, Solomon fell asleep and began to dream. ". . . the LORD appeared to Solomon . . . and God said, Ask what I shall give thee." (I Kings 3:5)

Solomon was probably most pleased to have such an opportunity. He replied, "I don't feel that I know how to be a good king." He then asked, "Give therefore thy servant an understanding heart to judge thy people, that I may discern between good and bad. . . ." (I Kings 3:9) The Lord was pleased with the young king's request and gave him just what he asked for. Solomon became one of the world's most famous men. Do you know why? Because he was known as the wisest man who ever lived. That is why even today we say of someone who makes a good decision, "He has the wisdom of Solomon."

THINK ABOUT IT

Would you make the same choice Solomon made if you had the opportunity? Why?

A WISE JUDGE
I Kings Chapter 3

One of the best examples of Solomon's wisdom is shown in an experience which occurred when two women came to him for judgment. Each woman was tugging and pulling at a beautiful little infant, who was crying. Both claimed, "This little baby is mine, not hers!" The king was amazed that such a problem could arise.

He knew the baby could have only one mother and he could not believe that anyone would be so wicked as to try to steal another mother's baby. Solomon was faced with the challenge of deciding which of the two women was lying and which was telling the truth.

The people in the king's court may have said softly to one another, "What will the king do? Both women seem to be telling the truth. I'm glad the king has to decide and not me. How will he decide?" Solomon asked for silence. Then for several seconds he looked first at one woman and then the other. The wise king finally spoke with firmness, "Bring me a sword." (I Kings 3:24)

A servant turned and departed through an open door. It was his task to bring back the razor sharp blade.

Whispers were heard among the onlookers. "Why did he ask for a sword? What will he do with it? Will he kill the one who is lying?"

When the servant returned clutching the long sword, silence filled the room. Staring first at one woman and then at the other, Solomon sat in silence. Then, slowly fixing his eyes on the sword bearer, he commanded, "Divide the living child in two, and give half to the one, and half to the other." (I Kings 3:25)

Instantly one of the two women began to cry and said to King Solomon, "O my lord, give her the living child. . . ." She fell on her knees and begged the king not to kill the baby. Then the other woman spoke loudly and said, ". . . divide *it*." (I Kings 3:26)

The wise king now knew which woman was the true mother. Looking at the sobbing mother, he said to his servant, "Give her the living child. . . ." (I Kings 3:27)

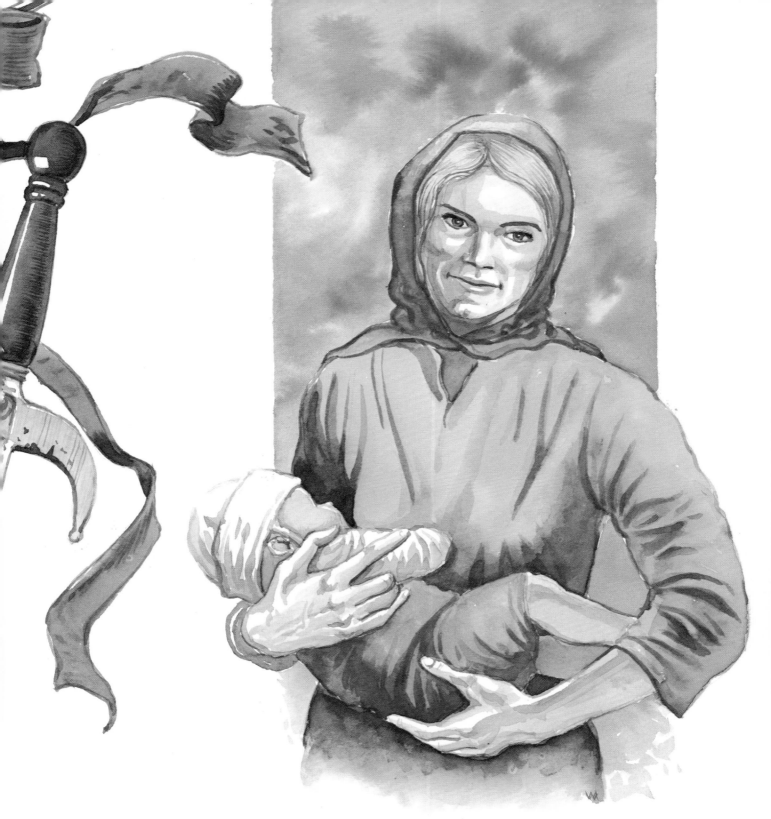

As the story of the two women and the baby was told throughout the kingdom, all the people were glad that they had such a great and wise leader.

Using the wisdom God had given him, Solomon ". . . spake three thousand proverbs [wise sayings]: and his songs were a thousand and five." (I Kings 4:32) Many of these are written in the books of Proverbs and Ecclesiastes in the Bible.

FULFILLING A DREAM
I Kings Chapters 6-8

Solomon's wisdom made it possible for him to do many mighty things. He taught his people how to build highways, great ships, and beautiful buildings. Under his leadership many people became rich and moved from tents into fine homes made of stone. The nation of Israel was truly becoming one of the great and rich kingdoms of the world.

As the beloved king sat in his beautiful palace, he often thought of David, his father. He remembered how King David had often spoken of his desire to build a temple for the Lord.

David had told Solomon, "I cannot build a temple because my hands have been bloodied by many wars. When I am gone, you must build the temple of which I have dreamed."

The time had come for Solomon to carry out the wishes of his father. He announced throughout all the land that very soon a beautiful temple would be built on the top of a hill in the city of Jerusalem.

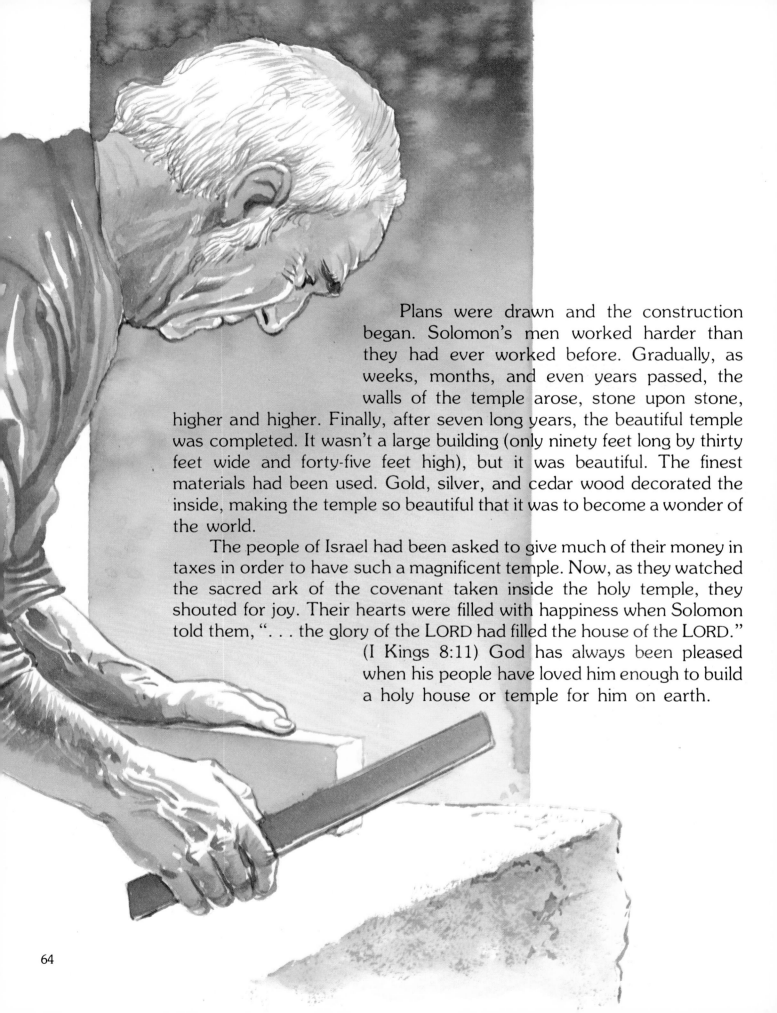

Plans were drawn and the construction began. Solomon's men worked harder than they had ever worked before. Gradually, as weeks, months, and even years passed, the walls of the temple arose, stone upon stone, higher and higher. Finally, after seven long years, the beautiful temple was completed. It wasn't a large building (only ninety feet long by thirty feet wide and forty-five feet high), but it was beautiful. The finest materials had been used. Gold, silver, and cedar wood decorated the inside, making the temple so beautiful that it was to become a wonder of the world.

The people of Israel had been asked to give much of their money in taxes in order to have such a magnificent temple. Now, as they watched the sacred ark of the covenant taken inside the holy temple, they shouted for joy. Their hearts were filled with happiness when Solomon told them, ". . . the glory of the LORD had filled the house of the LORD." (I Kings 8:11) God has always been pleased when his people have loved him enough to build a holy house or temple for him on earth.

HUMILITY AND WISDOM
I Kings Chapter 10

Because of the beautiful temple and the great deeds of Solomon, his fame and wisdom were known far and wide. When the Queen of Sheba heard of the beauty of the city of Jerusalem and the temple, she traveled many days to see them for herself. After visiting many parts in Solomon's kingdom, she said to him in amazement, "I was told how great your kingdom is. Now that I have seen it, I know that what I heard before was not half as wonderful as what I have just seen." Pride filled Solomon's heart as the beautiful queen praised him for all that he had done. The king, who had been humble before, was now becoming very proud and beginning to feel he no longer needed any special help from God.

The nation of Israel, which had come from slavery in Egypt many years before, was now a mighty kingdom—the envy of the world. God was pleased with his chosen people, but he knew Solomon had changed. Satan, on the other hand, was making use of Solomon's pride and carefully laying plans to destroy all the good that this great king could do.

King Solomon was now so famous that many other kings wanted him to marry their daughters. This made his pride grow even more. He agreed to these marriages and soon had hundreds of wives. Satan's sad seeds of destruction were planted and beginning to grow.

PLEASING PEOPLE RATHER THAN THE LORD
I Kings Chapter 11

Many of Solomon's wives did not believe in the true God of Israel. Forgetting his former love for God, the unfaithful king tried to make each wife happy. To do this he would worship with each wife in a different manner. Sometimes he would foolishly bow down to false gods or idols. Somehow he seemed to hear the voice of Satan saying, "It doesn't matter how you worship. It isn't as important to please God as it is to please your wives."

As the people watched the king do these things, many followed his example and did the same. Thus the Israelites forgot their true God and began to worship false gods. From the beginning Satan had fought against God's plans and now he was very pleased to see what was happening. He continued encouraging the people to forget the God who had led them out of Egypt, had parted the Red Sea, and had performed many miracles to help them. The king wanted to be popular with the people, so he did nothing to show them the error of their ways.

As the years passed, Solomon turned away from God more and more. He began to lose the great gift of wisdom with which the Lord had blessed him. He made poor decisions and the people complained that he was no longer a wise leader. They also began to feel that the taxes they had to pay to him were too heavy a burden for them to bear.

Some probably wished that the king, who had once been so wise, would die so that they could have a better king. That wish finally came true and the man, who at one time had been the wisest man in history, died. Behind him he left a kingdom that was ready to crumble because of the foolishness of his later life.

THINK ABOUT IT

1. Wisdom is the ability to see how a decision made today will affect us in the future. Why do we need God's help if we are to be wise?
2. Why doesn't Satan want us to be wise?
3. How did Solomon lose his wisdom?

LOVE AND HAPPINESS TO MISERY
I Kings Chapter 12

During his reign as king, Solomon had gone from being wise to being foolish. At the same time the kingdom had gone from one of love and trust to one of hate and suspicion. Is it any wonder that after Solomon's death the once-strong nation was split into two weak kingdoms? The southern portion was called the kingdom of Judah. It was made up of two of the twelve tribes. The kingdom of Israel was in the nothern area and was composed of the other ten tribes of Israel.

The people of the northern kingdom (Israel) and the southern kingdom (Judah) each loved the false gods of Satan more than the true God. Satan rejoiced, for he knew that when God's chosen people follow false gods they soon become wicked and unhappy. He was right, and the Israelites, weakened by their sins, struggled to survive against their enemies.

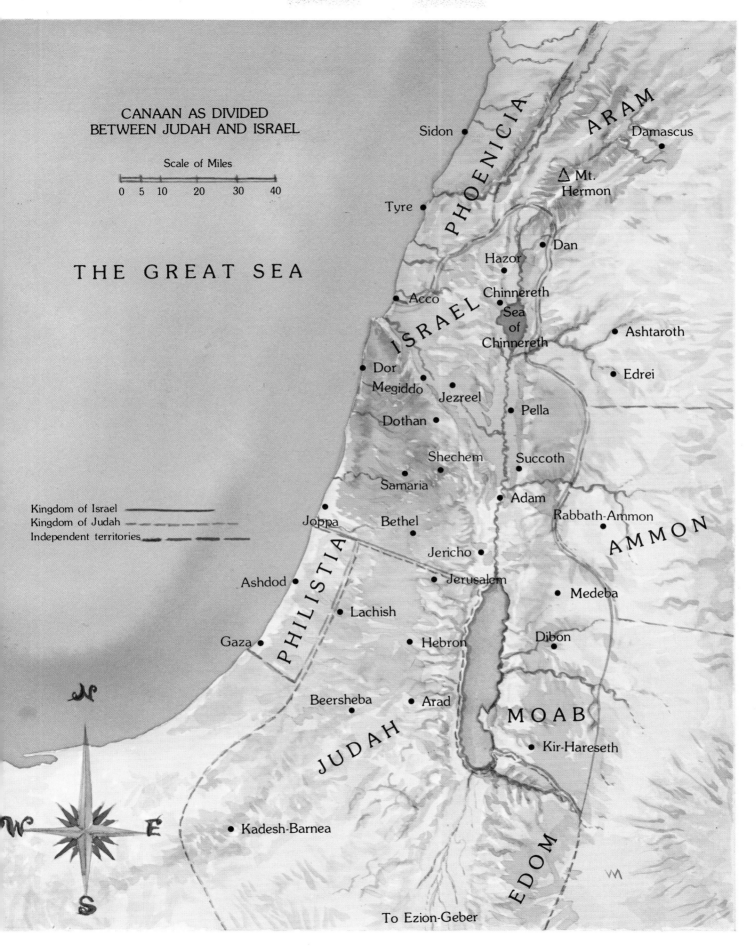

CANAAN AS DIVIDED
BETWEEN JUDAH AND ISRAEL

Scale of Miles

0 5 10   20   30   40

THE GREAT SEA

Kingdom of Israel ————
Kingdom of Judah — — —
Independent territories — — —

PHOENICIA

ARAM

Sidon

Damascus

△ Mt.
Hermon

Tyre

Dan

Hazor

Chinnereth

Acco

ISRAEL

Sea
of
Chinnereth

Ashtaroth

Dor

Edrei

Megiddo

Jezreel

Pella

Dothan

Shechem

Succoth

Samaria

Adam

Rabbath-Ammon

Joppa

Bethel

AMMON

Jericho

Ashdod

Jerusalem

PHILISTIA

Medeba

Lachish

Dibon

Gaza

Hebron

Beersheba

Arad

MOAB

Kir-Hareseth

JUDAH

Kadesh-Barnea

EDOM

To Ezion-Geber

75

WANTED: A STRONG LEADER

Again God's chosen people (the descendants of Abraham, Isaac, and Jacob) needed a great leader. But alas, there was no such leader in any of their cities. It was at this time that somewhere out in the wilderness a baby was born. The mother, holding the infant in her arms, asked the proud father, "What shall we name him?" The warm and quick reply was, "He shall be called Elijah, which means, 'My God is Jehovah.'"

Far away from city life the young boy, Elijah, grew up living close to nature. He loved the sunshine and the rain. He prayed often and received answers to his prayers. He soon became aware that he had a mighty mission to perform. Perhaps he could bring the twelve tribes together into one kingdom. More than that, he hoped that in some way he could inspire his people to return to a true belief in the God of Israel.

THINK ABOUT IT

Which was more important: to unite the two kingdoms or to inspire the people to once again worship God? Why?

THE MISSION BEGINS
I Kings Chapter 17

The years passed. Elijah grew and became a young man, learning well the lessons taught to him by the Lord. Finally the time came to act. Out of the wilderness and into the city where King Ahab and his wicked wife, Jezebel, lived came Elijah.

Laughter filled the air as Elijah entered the city, went to the marketplace, and announced to a curious audience, "As the LORD God of Israel liveth . . . there shall not be dew nor rain these years, but according to my word." (I Kings 17:1) Some of the people may have mockingly asked, "You mean you can control the rain?" while others laughed. As the Lord had instructed him, Elijah turned and, almost as suddenly as he had appeared, returned again into the wilderness.

A full year passed, but no rain fell. The grass dried and disappeared and the trees became barren and brown. Some thought back to the day they had laughed at the strange prophet for claiming he could control the rain. Could his words have been true?

Concerned, King Ahab began a search for the prophet who had come and gone so long ago.

There was little chance of finding the prophet Elijah for he was far away by a little stream that flowed down a rugged canyon into the Jordan River.

In this secluded hideout Elijah once again talked with God. The Lord sent ravens to be his companions. Every time these faithful, beautiful birds came near, they brought Elijah tender morsels of food.

Each day as he drank from the waters of the brook Cherith, he noticed there was less and less water flowing across the rocks. Nearly three years had passed since the last drop of water had fallen from the sky and splashed upon the land. Often Elijah wondered, "How much longer must I prepare? How much longer must I wait?" Then one day the Lord finally spoke and told the great prophet to leave that place and his friends the ravens and travel to a city called Zarephath.

THINK ABOUT IT

1. What does this story teach us about how God supports his servants?
2. Why did Elijah have to wait so long before he could continue with his mission?

NEVER-ENDING FOOD
I Kings Chapter 17

The journey was long, hot, and dry. Elijah was hungry and painfully thirsty as he approached the city where the Lord had told him to go.

As God had promised, Elijah was met there by a widow. He asked her for food, but she exclaimed how poor she was, having just a little food for herself and her young son. Elijah sensed she was a good woman and promised her that if she would take her little bit of flour and oil and make him a small cake, she would always have enough food.

Faithfully, she left him and went to her house. She scraped up the tiny bit of flour, poured in the last of the oil, and cooked the small cake. She then had the honor of providing food for this great prophet. Because of her faith in the words of Elijah, the barrel was never again empty of flour, and oil could always be found in the jars. ". . . and she, and he, and her house, did eat *many* days." (I Kings 17:15)

THINK ABOUT IT

If a servant of the Lord asked you for food, would you feed him? Why?

FROM DEATH TO LIFE
I Kings Chapter 17

Because of the faith and kindness of this widow, Elijah lived in her home for many days. The woman's young son and Elijah became dear friends. Then one day without warning the lad was stricken with a serious illness. It quickly became worse until the boy could hardly breathe. Within moments he was dead.

The sorrowful mother immediately called for Elijah. The prophet, hearing the alarm in her voice, hurried down from the loft where he was staying. As he gazed at the dead boy, the sobbing woman told him what had happened.

"Now by this I know that thou *art* a man of God. . . ." (I Kings 17:24) She was right. Elijah was indeed a mighty man of God.

THINK ABOUT IT

How did Elijah raise this boy from the dead? Is it possible for people today to perform such mighty miracles?

Elijah spoke words of comfort to the widow. Then he silently took the lifeless boy into his arms and returned up the stairs to the loft. "And he stretched himself upon the child three times, and cried unto the LORD, and said, O LORD my God, I pray thee, let this child's soul come into him again. And the LORD heard the voice of Elijah; and the soul of the child came into him again, and he revived." (I Kings 17:21, 22)

A few minutes later Elijah brought the living child down the stairs. Imagine the joy of the widow upon seeing her son alive again! She cried out to Elijah:

THE CONTEST
I Kings Chapter 18

It had been three long, dry, miserable years since the last rain had fallen. King Ahab, Queen Jezebel, and all their people knew that if it didn't rain soon, they would die. They had been pleading and sacrificing to their false god Baal in hope of relief. Elijah, who had been patiently waiting, was told by the Lord to come out of hiding, find Ahab, and tell him that rain was coming.

Elijah, the fearless prophet, wanted the people to know of the Lord's power. Thus he told Ahab to bring all the people together at Mount Carmel. Thousands came and they made a noticeable murmur when Elijah, who had become a legend, appeared on a small hill overlooking the large crowd.

Many called for silence when they saw the prophet was about to speak. Elijah's voice was loud and had the power that only a prophet can have. He cried out, "How long halt ye between two opinions? if the LORD *be* God, follow him: but if Baal, *then* follow him." (I Kings 18:21)

Silence filled the air as the people considered this great challenge. Then Elijah spoke again. He announced a contest between the power of God, led by Elijah, and the power of Satan, demonstrated by the four hundred and fifty evil prophets of the false god Baal.

The excitement grew as Elijah challenged the prophets of Baal to prepare an animal, cut it into pieces, and lay it on the wood of Baal's altar. There was to be no fire under it.

Elijah also prepared a bullock, laid it on wood, and put no fire under it. Then he said, "And call ye on the name of your gods, and I will call on the name of the LORD: and the God that answereth by fire, let him be God. And all the people answered and said, It is well spoken." (I Kings 18:24)

The worshippers of Baal were given the first chance to bring down heavenly fire. What went on in the minds of the priests of Baal as they prepared their altar is not known. One of them might have whispered to another, "I hope this works, but I don't see how it possibly can."

The frantic priests knew that unless something happened they would suffer public disgrace. Nothing did happen. Hours came and went as Elijah kept shouting, "What is wrong? Cry louder. Maybe your god is talking to someone else, maybe he is looking for something, or maybe he is on a journey. Perhaps he is asleep. Wake him up."

Finally, worn out by their long efforts and knowing there was no hope, the priests of Baal gave up. No fire had come.

Now it was Elijah's turn. The people, weary of the long time spent by the priests of Baal, shouted with new excitement, "It is the prophet's turn. Let us see what his God can do."

Elijah poured twelve barrels of water on the altar to make the task even more difficult. Then he was ready. The people probably whispered, "He couldn't have done it before, but with all that water there is no way fire can come down now."

Elijah prayed, "Hear me, O LORD, hear me, that this people may know that thou *art* the LORD God. . . . Then the fire of the LORD fell, and consumed the burnt sacrifice, and the wood, and the stones, and the dust, and licked up the water that *was* in the trench. And when all the people saw *it* . . . they said, The

LORD he *is* the God; the LORD, *he is* the God." (I Kings 18:37-39) Elijah's heart was filled with joy. God had kept his promises. Surely now the people would follow the true God.

As the people stood in wonder talking of the great miracle which they had seen, a cloud appeared on the horizon. The winds blew and in a few minutes the smell of rain was in the air. Once again the heavens, which had been sealed closed by Elijah, were opened. Pleasant, lifesaving rain drenched the parched earth.

THINK ABOUT IT

1. Would you like to have seen this great contest? Why?
2. Do you think Elijah had a sense of humor? Why?

THE MISSION ENDS
I Kings Chapter 19, II Kings Chapter 2

During his lifetime much more happened to Elijah. Truly his God was Jehovah. One time as he was praying to know the will of God, he heard a great and strong wind break rocks into pieces. However, the Lord was not in the wind. Then he saw an earthquake, but the Lord was not in the earthquake either. A fire came next, but the Lord was not even in the fire. ". . . and after the fire a still small voice." (I Kings 19:12)

Thus the Lord spoke to his mighty prophet through a still, small voice. A voice that could only be heard with the heart. A voice through which the God of Israel will also speak to anyone who will listen.

Sometime later, after choosing Elisha to take his place, the prophet Elijah was taken up into heaven in a fiery chariot. Some miracles he had performed during his lifetime included: controlling the rain, causing food to replace itself, raising a boy from the dead, bringing down fire from heaven, and making a powerful king and a wicked queen fear him.

Hyacinth: A native plant of the Eastern Mediterranean. It is thought to be the "lily" referred to in the Bible.

Surely his God was Jehovah. Elijah demon-strated to all that we should never halt between two opinions, nor should we sit and watch, but we should know God. If we are on the Lord's side and follow him, we will surely win.

Elijah had begun the series of miraculous events that helped the people of Israel end their worship of the false god Baal and to once again worship the true God of Israel. Another prophet with a name somewhat similar, Elisha, finished the work begun by his great teacher, Elijah. As Elijah was taken to heaven in a chariot, Elisha alone stood watching. He remembered when he had first met Elijah, how he had prayed that he might have a double portion of the old prophet's spirit. (II Kings 2:9)

In a way his prayer was answered. Although he wasn't as famous as Elijah, many of his works were in a sense twice as spectacular as were Elijah's.

He helped a widow, whose sons were about to become slaves, to pay off her debts. She became rich by the miraculous power he gave her to fill many vases of oil from one vase. (II Kings 4:2-7)

He blessed a kind woman who had not been able to have children, and she bore a fine son. When the son was a small boy, he suddenly died. The mother came to Elisha and he went to the boy and restored him back to life. (II Kings 4:14-35)

116

He told a mighty general with the incurable disease called leprosy to bathe seven times in the Jordan River and he would be healed.

The general at first thought Elisha's advice was foolish. But through the encouragement of his servant he bathed seven times and was miraculously healed. (II Kings 5:1-14)

He told the army officers of his time how to win battles, and
when they followed his advice, they won. He could see, by his great

faith, the mighty spiritual armies of God that were there to protect Israel. (II Kings 6:8-23)

120

Elisha finally chose a king named Jehu, who destroyed all the priests of Baal. (II Kings 10:18-28)

At last Elisha's work was done. No one except Jesus Christ performed more miracles than this kind, magnificent prophet. Elisha indeed had had a double portion of Elijah's spirit. What Elijah began, Elisha finished. The people of Israel were once again strong in their faith of the almighty God of their ancestors Abraham, Isaac, Jacob, Joseph, Moses, and Joshua.

THE RICH OR THE POOR
Amos Chapters 1-9

"I'm better than you are because I have more money than you!" shouted a richly dressed Israelite at a fellow countryman, whose shabby clothes scarcely covered his hungry body.

At this time Baal worship was gone. Elijah and Elisha had helped see to that. But now, 765 years before the birth of Christ, a new trouble was in the land. Satan was causing some to feel in their hearts that they were better than others.

Instead of worshipping Baal, the people worshipped money and loved themselves more than they loved the true God of Israel.

God knew that Satan could destroy God's people by causing some to feel they were better than others because they were rich. Thus, far out in a little country town named Tekoa, God inspired a humble shepherd named Amos, and he became a mighty prophet.

One day Amos walked down a long, muddy road to the city Bethel. He was bringing with him some wool to sell at the marketplace. As he walked along, his mind was not on how much money he would get for the wool. He had a greater purpose than that, for he was going to give a speech. Over and over again he kept thinking of the words he would say to the self-loving, rich people who lived there.

Amos was able to sell his wool quickly. As he walked about watching the people, he felt sick inside. He saw many finely dressed people proudly offering insincere sacrifices to the Lord, yet moments later saying cruel words to someone poorly dressed. The prophet could hardly wait to shout out the message which God had placed in his heart.

Amos finally found just the right place amidst a large crowd. Walking back against a doorway above some stairs, he shouted, "Listen to me!" At first he praised the power of Israel. All who heard shouted, "You are right. We are

indeed a great nation." But then the darkly suntanned face took on a stern look as he quoted the Lord: "I hate, I despise your feast days. . . . Though ye offer me burnt offerings . . . I will not accept *them*. . . ." (Amos 5:21, 22)

At first the people talked among themselves. Then one by one they became quiet until the only voice heard was that of the prophet. Suddenly one man shouted, "What is he saying? He is a mad man!" Amos was not disturbed by the unkind remark. He continued telling them that they must repent and treat all people alike, both rich and poor, or they would be destroyed.

Soon a group of rich leaders gathered and said, "We can't let this man speak this way. It could cause much trouble." Another said, "Let's get him and throw him out of the city." The group called for some city guards and these men told the prophet to quit speaking. Amos didn't mind. He was giving the message God had sent him to give. He was led away by the guards.

Saddened that the leaders had not seemed to listen, but satisfied that God had inspired him, Amos walked down the lonely road that would take him home.

He had said what he knew he needed to say. His voice had been God's voice. At home he wrote more of God's words, and what he wrote will live forever as the book of Amos.

PREVIEW OF THINGS TO COME

The next volume will be the last one containing stories from the Old Testament.

We will read of the fall of the northern kingdom, as ten of the twelve tribes of Israel are carried away captive, never to return to the Promised Land.

The prophet Isaiah was a statesman and prophet and mingled with the kings. He will prophesy of the future—even to our day. He will prophesy that Christ will be born.

Next comes Jeremiah and his sad but powerful mission. The people of the southern kingdom, Judah, refuse to repent. They too are captured and taken from their homes to another land.

We will learn of the prophet Ezekiel and his visions of hope. We will study about and love the loyal and faithful Daniel. We will read of the bravery of Queen Esther, the patience of Job, the adventures of Jonah and the whale, and finally of the last prophet of the Old Testament, Malachi.

The sixth volume will be another exciting and faith promoting experience for each of us.